Grow a Backbone and Walk out of an Abusive Marriage

Kayumba David & Rachael Nyarangi

Grow a Backbone and Walk out of an Abusive Marriage

1

Kayumba David and Rachael Nyarangi

Published by Kayumba David, 2024.

GROW A BACKBONE AND WALK OUT OF AN ABUSIVE MARRIAGE

First edition. November 4, 2024.

Copyright © 2024 Kayumba David and Rachael Nyarangi.

ISBN: 979-8224396245

Written by Kayumba David and Rachael Nyarangi.

Also by Kayumba David

1
Grow a Backbone and Walk out of an Abusive Marriage

Standalone
Cry Africa The Western Guide on How Not to Fail the Continent
Grow a Backbone and Walk out of an Abusive Marriage
Hope and Healing: A Chaplain's Handbook
Visas: The Irony of Freedom
A Meeting with Majesty: The King's Call to Humanity
Visas: The Irony of Freedom
Love Beyond Time A Comedy of Divine Connection
Silent Complicity: State Sovereignty, Global Inaction, and the
Rwandan Genocide
Bridging the Rift: A Pacifist Vision for the Israel-Palestine Future
Thanks to Calvary: A Salvific Treatise on the Cross
The centuries old swindlers
Harvesting Illusions: The Global Greed and the Pan-African Paradox
Hope and Recovery - A Chaplain's Handbook
The Only Crying God in all the Universe
LGBTQ Debunked by Natural Law
The Scandal of Gentleness: Who Was Jesus?
The Day of Reckoning: Leadership, Justice, and Divine Accountability

Watch for more at www.zcews.org.

Also by Rachael Nyarangi

1

Grow a Backbone and Walk out of an Abusive Marriage

Standalone

Grow a Backbone and Walk out of an Abusive Marriage
Love Beyond Time A Comedy of Divine Connection

Preface

This book is a testament to the countless women who have endured the unbearable and found the strength to reclaim their lives. The inspiration to write this guide comes from the many experiences of suffering women, especially in Africa, where the acceptance of abuse is often perpetuated by societal casuistry and deep-seated traditional biases against women.

In many African societies, women are often taught from a young age to accept male dominance and endure pain silently. Cultural and traditional norms frequently intertwine, creating an environment where abuse is not just tolerated but expected. The modern state, which should be a sanctuary of support, sometimes tends to be keep a blind eye and perpetuate this suffering. This toxic blend of cultural and traditional indoctrination can make it incredibly difficult for women to recognize abuse for what it is, let alone find the courage to leave.

I have seen firsthand the devastating effects of this systemic oppression. I have heard the stories of women who have been beaten, belittled, and betrayed, yet told to remain steadfast and obedient. These women, who live under the constant shadow of fear and degradation, have inspired me to write this book. It is a guide for those who feel trapped, a beacon of hope for those who believe they have no way out.

This book is not just about leaving an abusive marriage; it is about reclaiming your life and finding your true self. It is about understanding that no cultural or religious doctrine should ever condone your suffering. It is about recognizing that you deserve love, respect, and happiness. Through practical advice, emotional support, and a touch of humor, this guide aims to empower you to take the necessary steps towards freedom.

You are not alone in this journey. Many women have walked this path before you, breaking free from their chains and building lives filled with joy and dignity. This book is dedicated to them and to you, the brave souls ready to take control of your destiny.

Welcome to your new life. It's time to embrace your strength, reclaim your power, and walk out with your head held high. You are the hero of your own story, and this is the beginning of a beautiful new chapter.

Acknowledgements

I want to acknowledge the courage and resilience of Rachael Nyarangi and all the women who have shared their stories with me. Your experiences have deeply moved me and have been the driving force behind this book. I also want to thank the support networks, both formal and informal, that have helped these women find their strength.

To the countless women who continue to fight for their freedom and dignity, this book is for you. May it serve as a guide and a source of strength as you embark on your journey to reclaim your life.

With deep respect and solidarity,

4

Introduction: From Chains to Freedom

Welcome to the journey from chains to freedom—a path that, while daunting, is paved with the promise of liberation and renewal. This book, "How to Grow a Backbone and Walk Out: The Sarcastic Guide to Escaping Your Abusive Marriage," is crafted for those who find themselves in the harrowing grip of an abusive relationship, often compounded by cultural and religious norms that attempt to justify their suffering.

For many women, the chains of abuse are not only physical but deeply embedded in the cultural and religious fabric of their lives. In places where traditional beliefs and religious doctrines can dictate personal worth and societal roles, escaping an abusive relationship can seem like an insurmountable challenge. These deeply entrenched systems often perpetuate the myth that enduring abuse is a sign of virtue, sacrificing individual well-being on the altar of misguided principles.

This guide emerges from a profound concern for those who have been ensnared by such chains. It recognizes that the journey to freedom is not just about physical escape but about reclaiming your dignity, self-worth, and the right to live a life free from fear and oppression. This book is not merely a manual for leaving; it is a call to arms for reclaiming your identity and your life.

You may have been told that enduring abuse is a part of your duty or that you must suffer in silence. You might have been led to believe that your worth is tied to how much pain you can endure. This guide challenges those falsehoods with a blend of practical advice and unapologetic sarcasm. It aims to strip away the illusions and reveal the truth: you deserve respect, love, and happiness, and no cultural or religious dogma has the right to deny you that.

Our approach here combines a realistic perspective with a touch of humor, because sometimes a little sarcasm can be a powerful tool in reclaiming one's sense of self. We will explore the red flags of abuse, offer strategies for escaping with style, and provide practical steps for building a new life. But beyond the tactics, this guide is a celebration of your courage and an affirmation of your right to live freely.

As you embark on this journey, remember that you are not alone. Countless women have walked this path before you, and countless more will follow. Each step you take toward freedom is a testament to your strength and resilience. Embrace the process, trust in your worth, and know that liberation is not just a dream—it's your right.

Welcome to your new life, where you are the hero of your own story, and the chains that once bound you are nothing but a distant memory.

Inspiration Behind This Guide

The inspiration for "How to Grow a Backbone and Walk Out: The Sarcastic Guide to Escaping Your Abusive Marriage" springs from a profound concern for the countless women trapped in cycles of abuse, particularly in contexts where cultural and religious constraints amplify their suffering. Observing the experiences of women in various parts of the world, especially in Africa, where deeply ingrained traditions and religious doctrines often perpetuate abuse, highlighted the urgent need for a resource that blends practical advice with a bold, liberating perspective.

Religious teachings and cultural norms have, for too long, been manipulated to justify the subjugation of women, masking their pain under the guise of spiritual duty or moral obligation. This guide emerges from a commitment to dismantling these harmful interpretations and advocating for a life where every woman is empowered to seek and secure her freedom.

In writing this book, I sought to offer not just a roadmap to escape but a reminder of the inherent worth and strength within every woman. Through a mix of candid advice, sarcastic humor, and unwavering support, this guide aims to help women reclaim their lives, challenge oppressive norms, and embrace their true potential. This work is a testament to the belief that liberation is a right, not a privilege, and that every woman deserves to live free from abuse and full of dignity.

Chapter 1

So, You're Married to a Jerk

Welcome, brave soul, to the first step in acknowledging that your partner is, indeed, a first-class jerk. This guide isn't here to sugarcoat anything. Let's face it: if your marriage feels like a never-ending episode of "Survivor" where the only prize is more misery, it's time for a change. But fear not, sarcasm is here to guide you through this tumultuous journey.

Recognizing the Reality

Admitting that you're married to an abusive partner is a monumental step. It's not just about acknowledging that your partner is a jerk; it's about understanding that you deserve better. In many parts of the world, particularly in Africa, cultural and religious beliefs can make this realization incredibly difficult. You might have been raised to accept male dominance and to believe that suffering is part of a woman's lot in life. These beliefs can be deeply ingrained, making it hard to see your situation for what it truly is: unacceptable.

Cultural and Religious Chains

Let's talk about these chains. Many cultures in Africa emphasize the submissiveness of women and the dominance of men. From a young age, girls are taught to be obedient, to serve their husbands, and to bear their burdens silently. Religious teachings might reinforce these ideas, suggesting that a woman's role is to endure and support her husband, no matter the cost to her own well-being.

However, it's crucial to understand that no cultural norm or religious doctrine should ever condone abuse. The sanctity of marriage does not mean sacrificing your safety and happiness. Challenging these deeply held beliefs can be daunting, but it's necessary for your survival and well-being.

The Sacred Duty to Reject Abuse

Here's a truism that you must hold onto tightly: No religious dogma should be relied upon to justify or perpetuate your suffering. It is your holy duty to reject both cultural and religious tenets that subject you to abuse, including beatings, insults, neglect, rape, and humiliation. Religion and culture should uplift and protect you, not imprison you in a cycle of pain and degradation.

The Reality Check

Let's break it down with a bit of sarcasm, shall we? Imagine this: Your partner is the star of a never-ending drama series called "The Misery Chronicles." Every episode features new ways to belittle you, control you, and make you feel worthless. And guess what? There's no season finale in sight.

But here's the kicker: you didn't sign up for this show. You didn't take vows to become the punching bag or the emotional dumping ground. Marriage is supposed to be a partnership, not a hostage situation. If you're spending your days walking on eggshells, fearing the next outburst, it's time to change the script.

Identifying the Abuse

Recognizing abuse isn't always straightforward. Abuse comes in many forms, and it's essential to understand that it's not limited to physical violence. Abuse can be emotional, psychological, and financial, each leaving deep scars. Here are some red flags to look out for:

1. Emotional Abuse

Emotional abuse is often insidious, slowly chipping away at your self-worth and confidence. It involves:

Constant Criticism: Your partner frequently criticizes you, pointing out flaws and making you feel like you can never do anything right. This criticism can be about your appearance, abilities, decisions, or even your personality.

Belittling: They make sarcastic comments or jokes at your expense, often in public, to humiliate you. This belittling behavior can make you feel small and insignificant.

Manipulation: Emotional manipulators twist situations to make you feel guilty or responsible for their bad behavior. They might use tactics like guilt-tripping, playing the victim, or giving you the silent treatment to control your actions and emotions.

Undermining Your Self-Esteem: Over time, constant emotional abuse can erode your self-esteem, making you doubt your worth and capabilities. You might start to believe that you deserve the abuse or that you can't survive without your partner.

2. Physical Abuse

Physical abuse is perhaps the most obvious form of abuse, but it can be minimized or excused in the context of cultural or religious beliefs. It includes:

Hitting, Slapping, or Pushing: Any form of physical violence, no matter how minor it may seem, is unacceptable. Physical abuse often escalates over time, becoming more frequent and severe.

Using Physical Intimidation: Your partner might use their physical presence to intimidate you, blocking your way, looming over you, or using gestures that threaten violence.

Forced Confinement: Preventing you from leaving the house, locking you in a room, or restricting your movement within the home.

Threats of Violence: Even if they don't follow through, threats of physical harm are a form of abuse designed to instill fear and maintain control.

3. Psychological Abuse

Psychological abuse, also known as mental or emotional abuse, involves behaviors that manipulate your sense of reality and autonomy. It includes:

Gaslighting: This manipulative tactic makes you question your reality. Your partner might deny events that you know happened, make you doubt your memory, or insist that you're overreacting or imagining things. Over time, gaslighting can make you feel confused and unsure of your perceptions.

Intimidation: Using threats, menacing looks, or aggressive behaviors to instill fear. Your partner might destroy property, hurt pets, or make threats about what they'll do if you leave or tell anyone about the abuse.

Isolation: They might isolate you from friends, family, and other support networks. This can involve controlling who you see, monitoring your communications, or spreading lies about you to turn others against you.

Emotional Blackmail: Using guilt, fear, or obligation to control you. They might threaten to harm themselves if you leave or accuse you of not loving them if you don't comply with their demands.

4. Financial Abuse

Financial abuse is a less recognized but equally damaging form of abuse. It involves controlling your ability to acquire, use, and maintain financial resources. It includes:

Controlling Access to Money: Your partner might control all the household finances, giving you an allowance or requiring you to account for every penny spent. They might withhold money for essentials, forcing you to beg for basic needs.

Preventing You from Working: They might forbid you from getting a job, sabotage your work opportunities, or harass you at your workplace. This ensures you remain financially dependent on them.

Taking Your Earnings: If you do work, they might take your earnings, leaving you with no control over your income. This can make it impossible to save money to leave or to feel financially secure.

Creating Financial Dependence: They might make financial decisions without consulting you, incur debt in your name, or destroy your credit. This makes it difficult for you to gain financial independence and leave the relationship.

Recognizing These Red Flags

These forms of abuse can exist in any combination, and they often escalate over time. Recognizing these red flags is the first step in understanding that you are in an abusive relationship. It's crucial to remember that abuse is never your fault, and you deserve a life free from fear and control. Identifying the abuse is not just about recognizing the signs; it's about empowering yourself to take the necessary steps to seek help and reclaim your life.

By understanding and identifying the various forms of abuse, you can begin to see the patterns and realize that what you are experiencing is not normal or acceptable. This awareness is the first step towards finding the strength to break free and seek a life of dignity and respect.

The Courage to Acknowledge

It takes immense courage to admit that you're in an abusive marriage. This is not just a casual realization; it's a profound acknowledgment that challenges your entire worldview. You might fear judgment from your community, rejection from family and friends, or even retaliation from your partner. These fears are compounded by cultural and religious pressures that often advocate for the sanctity of marriage above personal well-being. These pressures can make it seem easier to stay and endure the abuse rather than risk the unknown.

However, true bravery isn't about enduring pain; it's about standing up for yourself. It's about recognizing that you deserve love, respect, and happiness. By acknowledging the abuse, you're taking a monumental step toward reclaiming your life. This acknowledgment is not a sign of weakness but a powerful affirmation of your worth and dignity. It's an act of self-respect that defies the cultural and religious narratives that have kept you shackled.

The Power of Sarcasm

Now, why sarcasm? Because sometimes, a little humor can be a powerful weapon in the face of adversity. Sarcasm allows you to emotionally distance yourself from the situation, giving you a fresh perspective on the absurdity of your partner's behavior. It can transform your despair into defiance, and your helplessness into humor. By using sarcasm, you reclaim a sense of control and remind yourself that you're not the helpless victim your partner wants you to be.

Sarcasm helps you break down the facade of the abuser's power. When you can laugh at the ridiculousness of their attempts to control and belittle you, you strip away some of their power. It's a way to mentally and emotionally fortify yourself against their tactics, giving you the strength to move forward.

Moving Forward

This guide will provide you with practical steps to escape your abusive marriage, build a support system, and start a new life. It won't be easy; there will be obstacles and moments of doubt. But every step you take is a victory, a move closer to the life you deserve. You're not alone in this journey. Countless women have walked this path before you, breaking free from their chains and reclaiming their lives.

Remember, acknowledging that you're married to a jerk is just the beginning. It's the first, crucial step toward freedom. From here, you will learn how to build a support network, navigate the complexities of leaving, and rebuild your life on your own terms.

So buckle up, embrace your inner sarcasm, and get ready to take control of your life. You deserve nothing less. You are worthy of love, respect, and happiness, and it's time to fight for it. With every step forward, you're not just moving away from the pain; you're moving towards a future filled with possibility and hope. You have the strength within you to transform your life, and this guide is here to support you every step of the way.

Chapter 2

Admit That You're Not in a Lifetime Movie

Contrary to popular belief, your life is not a melodramatic TV movie where the abusive partner suddenly reforms after a heartfelt speech. Acknowledging this fact is crucial. Your partner is unlikely to have a miraculous change of heart, so it's time to stop hoping for one.

The Reality Check

In many melodramatic TV movies, the abusive partner sees the error of their ways after a dramatic confrontation or a tearful plea. They suddenly transform into a loving, supportive spouse, and the couple lives happily ever after. Unfortunately, real life doesn't work that way. These narratives are fictional, crafted for entertainment, and often perpetuate unrealistic expectations about change and redemption in abusive relationships.

Abuse is about power and control. Your partner's abusive behavior is deeply rooted in their need to dominate and control you. This behavior is not something that will vanish overnight with a simple heart-to-heart conversation. Real change requires deep self-awareness, a genuine desire to change, and extensive professional help, which most abusers are not willing to seek.

Letting Go of False Hope

Holding onto the hope that your partner will change can keep you trapped in a cycle of abuse. It's natural to want to believe that things will get better, especially when your partner occasionally shows kindness or remorse. These moments of apparent kindness can create a confusing dynamic known as the "cycle of abuse," where periods of relative calm and affection are interspersed with episodes of abuse. This cycle can make it incredibly difficult to leave, as you may cling to the hope that the good times will eventually outweigh the bad.

However, it's important to recognize that these moments of kindness do not negate the abuse. They are often part of the manipulative tactics used by abusers to maintain control over you. Letting go of the false hope that your partner will change is a painful but necessary step in your journey towards freedom.

The Illusion of Control

One of the most insidious aspects of abuse is the illusion of control it creates. You might believe that if you just behave differently, avoid certain triggers, or improve in some way, the abuse will stop. This belief is a trap. Abuse is not your fault, and nothing you do can change your partner's behavior. The responsibility for the abuse lies solely with the abuser.

The Myth of the Perfect Apology

Abusers often use apologies as a tool to manipulate and control. They might apologize profusely after an abusive episode, promising that it will never happen again. These apologies can be very convincing, especially when accompanied by tears and declarations of love. However, these apologies are often hollow, serving only to reset the cycle of abuse. True remorse is shown through consistent actions over time, not just words.

Understanding the Dynamics of Abuse

To fully grasp why change is unlikely, it's essential to understand the dynamics of abusive relationships. Abuse is about power and control, not about anger or loss of temper. Abusers use various tactics to maintain control, including:

- **Isolation:** Keeping you away from friends and family to weaken your support system.

- **Intimidation:** Using threats or aggressive behavior to instill fear.
- **Emotional Manipulation:** Undermining your self-esteem and making you doubt your perceptions.
- **Financial Control:** Limiting your access to money to increase your dependence.

These tactics are deliberate and calculated, making it clear that abuse is a choice, not a mistake. Abusers are often unwilling to relinquish this control, which is why expecting them to change without significant intervention is unrealistic.

The Power of Acceptance

Accepting that your partner is unlikely to change is liberating. It frees you from the burden of trying to fix an unfixable situation and allows you to focus on what you can control—your actions and your future. Acceptance doesn't mean giving up; it means redirecting your energy towards building a life free from abuse.

Moving Forward

Moving forward requires courage and support. Surround yourself with people who understand and validate your experiences. Seek out resources and professional help to guide you through the process of leaving and rebuilding your life. Remember, you are not alone. Many women have faced similar challenges and have successfully escaped abusive relationships.

In this journey, it's crucial to be kind to yourself. Acknowledge the strength it takes to face the reality of your situation and take steps towards change. Embrace your inner resilience and know that you deserve a life filled with respect, love, and happiness.

Conclusion

Admitting that you're not in a Lifetime movie is a pivotal step in your journey to freedom. It means letting go of false hopes and recognizing the reality of your situation. By doing so, you empower yourself to take control of your life and move towards a future free from abuse. Embrace this reality with courage and determination, knowing that you have the strength to overcome and thrive.

Chapter 3

Master the Art of Eye Rolling

Sarcasm is your new best friend. Master the art of eye-rolling to deal with the absurdities thrown your way. This will be your first act of defiance. Remember, each eye roll is a step towards reclaiming your sanity.

The Power of Sarcasm

Sarcasm is a subtle yet powerful form of resistance. When you're stuck in an abusive relationship, it can feel like your every action is controlled, monitored, and judged. Sarcasm offers a way to reclaim a bit of your power and sanity. It allows you to acknowledge the ridiculousness of your partner's behavior without directly confronting them, which can be crucial for your safety.

The Art of Eye Rolling

Eye-rolling is more than just a physical action; it's a symbolic gesture of defiance. Here's how mastering this simple act can help you:

Emotional Release: Rolling your eyes can provide an immediate release of frustration. It's a non-verbal way of expressing your disbelief and disdain for the absurdity you're facing.

Mental Distance: Each eye roll helps create a mental distance between you and the abuse. It's a small step towards seeing the situation from an outsider's perspective, which can help you understand that the problem lies with your partner, not you.

Reclaiming Power: Eye-rolling is a subtle form of rebellion. It's a way to assert your autonomy and show that you're not completely subdued. It's a reminder to yourself that you still have a voice, even if it's silent for now.

Practical Tips for Sarcasm and Eye-Rolling

Timing is Everything

Using sarcasm and eye-rolling effectively requires timing. You need to gauge when it's safe to use these tools. If your partner has a volatile temper, be cautious and ensure that your sarcasm doesn't provoke more aggression.

Subtlety is Key

The goal is to use sarcasm and eye-rolling to maintain your sanity and assert some control, not to escalate the situation. Keep your sarcasm subtle and your eye-rolls understated. This way, you can avoid direct confrontations while still giving yourself a small victory.

Internal Sarcasm

If overt sarcasm isn't safe, practice internal sarcasm. Mentally roll your eyes and think sarcastic thoughts. This internal dialogue can be just as effective in helping you cope with the daily absurdities without putting yourself at risk.

Examples of Sarcasm and Eye-Rolling

Situation: Your partner makes an unreasonable demand.

- **Internal Response:** Mentally roll your eyes and think, "Oh sure, because I'm a mind reader now."

Situation: Your partner criticizes you for something trivial.

- **Response:** Roll your eyes subtly and say, "Of course, I forgot you're perfect."

The Psychological Benefits

Using sarcasm and eye-rolling has psychological benefits:

1. **Stress Relief:** These small acts can help reduce stress by providing a safe outlet for your frustration.
2. **Maintaining Self-Respect:** Sarcasm can help you maintain your self-respect. It's a way to remind yourself that you recognize the absurdity and unacceptability of the abuse.
3. **Building Resilience:** Over time, these small acts of defiance can build your emotional resilience, making you stronger and more capable of taking bigger steps towards freedom.

Sarcasm as a Survival Tool

In an abusive relationship, survival often means finding ways to cope with the daily indignities and injustices. Sarcasm can be a survival tool, helping you to keep a part of yourself intact. It's a way to maintain your identity and remind yourself that you are more than the abuse you're enduring.

Moving Towards Action

While sarcasm and eye-rolling are useful coping mechanisms, they are just the beginning. They are small steps that can help you regain your sense of self and sanity, but they are not solutions. As you build your inner strength through these acts of defiance, start planning your larger strategy for leaving the abusive situation.

Conclusion

Mastering the art of eye-rolling and wielding sarcasm like a shield are your first steps in reclaiming your sanity. These small acts of defiance remind you that you still have power, even in the face of absurdity. Use them wisely and let them be the foundation upon which you build your path to freedom. Remember, every eye roll and sarcastic thought is a step towards regaining your life and sanity. You deserve respect, love, and happiness, and these small acts are the beginning of your journey to achieve them.

Your relationship is likely filled with red flags. It's time to document every single one. Make a list, and then, metaphorically, set it on fire. This exercise isn't just cathartic; it's also a stark reminder of why you need to leave.

Chapter 4

Recognizing the Red Flags

Red flags are warning signs that indicate something is wrong in your relationship. These can range from subtle behaviors that make you uncomfortable to overt acts of aggression. Recognizing these red flags is crucial because it helps you see the pattern of abuse clearly. Here are some common red flags to look out for:

1. **Controlling Behavior:** Your partner insists on knowing where you are at all times, dictates who you can and cannot see, and makes decisions for you.
2. **Extreme Jealousy:** They are overly possessive and constantly accuse you of infidelity without any basis.
3. **Isolation:** They isolate you from friends, family, and other support networks, making you increasingly dependent on them.
4. **Verbal Abuse:** They regularly insult, belittle, or criticize you, making you feel worthless.
5. **Physical Violence:** Any form of physical aggression, such as hitting, slapping, pushing, or restraining.
6. **Emotional Manipulation:** They use guilt, fear, and obligation to control you, often making you feel responsible for their behavior.
7. **Gaslighting:** They deny events, twist your words, and make you question your reality and sanity.
8. **Financial Control:** They control all the finances, give you an allowance, or forbid you from working, making you financially dependent on them.
9. **Threats and Intimidation:** They use threats of violence, harm, or abandonment to keep you in line.

10. **Disrespect for Boundaries:** They disregard your personal boundaries and privacy, often invading your personal space or demanding constant attention.

Documenting the Red Flags

Creating a detailed catalog of these red flags can be a powerful exercise. Here's how to go about it:

Step 1: Make a List

Start by listing every red flag you can think of. Be as detailed as possible. Write down specific incidents, what was said or done, how it made you feel, and any patterns you notice. This list will help you see the scope and severity of the abuse.

- **Example Entry:** "March 15th - He called me 'stupid' in front of our friends because I disagreed with him about politics. Felt humiliated and small."
- **Example Entry:** "April 2nd - He grabbed my arm and squeezed it hard during an argument. Left a bruise."

Step 2: Reflect on the Impact

Reflect on how these red flags have impacted your mental and physical health, self-esteem, and overall well-being. This reflection is crucial in understanding the full extent of the damage caused by the abuse.

- **Example Reflection:** "Constant criticism has made me doubt my abilities at work. I feel anxious and fearful even when he's not around."

Step 3: Metaphorically Set Them on Fire

Once you have your list, it's time for a symbolic act of release. Find a safe way to destroy the list. You could burn it in a controlled environment, shred it, or tear it up and throw it away. This act is not just symbolic but also cathartic. It represents your commitment to leaving the abuse behind and reclaiming your life.

The Cathartic Power of Letting Go

Destroying the list serves multiple purposes:

1. **Emotional Release:** It helps you release pent-up emotions and anger. It's a physical manifestation of letting go of the pain and trauma.
2. **Empowerment:** It empowers you to take control of your narrative. You're not just a victim; you're actively choosing to move forward.
3. **Clarity:** It reinforces the clarity you've gained from recognizing the red flags. It's a reminder of why you need to leave and what you deserve—respect, love, and happiness.

Using the List as Evidence

Before you set your list on fire, consider making a copy to keep as evidence. This documentation can be invaluable if you decide to take legal action, seek a restraining order, or need to explain your situation to a counselor or support group. Having a clear record of the abuse can strengthen your case and provide a solid foundation for seeking help.

Moving Forward

After you've metaphorically set the red flags on fire, it's time to focus on your next steps. Here are a few actions to consider:

1. **Seek Support:** Reach out to friends, family, or support groups who can provide emotional and practical support. Don't be afraid to ask for help.

2. **Professional Help:** Consider seeking help from a counselor or therapist who specializes in domestic abuse. They can provide you with the tools and strategies to cope with the trauma and plan your escape.

3. **Legal Advice:** If you feel it's safe to do so, consult with a legal professional to understand your rights and options for leaving the relationship. This might include filing for a restraining order or seeking custody of your children.

Conclusion

Cataloging the red flags in your relationship and setting them on fire is a powerful exercise in reclaiming your power and sanity. It helps you recognize the abuse, reflect on its impact, and symbolically release it. This process is a crucial step towards leaving the abusive relationship and building a life filled with respect, love, and happiness. Remember, you are not alone, and there is support available to help you through this journey. Take this step with courage and determination, knowing that you deserve a life free from abuse.

Chapter 5

Gather Your Wits (and Your Evidence)

Starting to gather evidence of the abuse you're enduring is not just for your peace of mind but also for crucial legal reasons. Documentation can be a lifesaver in court, providing the concrete proof you need to secure protection and support. Channel your inner detective and keep a detailed record of everything. This chapter will guide you through the process of collecting and safeguarding evidence.

Why Gathering Evidence is Essential

Gathering evidence serves several critical purposes:

1. **Legal Protection:** In legal proceedings, such as filing for a restraining order or seeking custody of children, having documented evidence of abuse can strengthen your case significantly.
2. **Validation:** Keeping a record can validate your experiences, helping you see the pattern of abuse clearly and reinforcing that what you're going through is not normal or acceptable.
3. **Emotional Strength:** Documenting incidents can empower you by giving you a tangible sense of control and action.

Types of Evidence to Collect

Evidence can come in many forms. Here are some key types to consider:

Physical Evidence

1. **Photographs:** Take photos of any physical injuries, damaged property, or other physical signs of abuse. Make sure to date these photos.

2. **Medical Records:** Visit a doctor for any injuries and keep records of your visits. Medical professionals can document the cause of injuries in their reports.
3. **Objects:** Preserve any objects that may have been used in an abusive incident, if it's safe to do so.

Written Evidence

1. **Journals:** Keep a detailed journal of every incident. Include dates, times, descriptions of the events, and any witnesses.
2. **Emails and Text Messages:** Save any abusive or threatening emails, text messages, or social media interactions. Screenshots can be useful here.
3. **Letters or Notes:** Keep any written threats or apologies from your partner.

Audio and Video Evidence

1. **Recordings:** If it's legal in your jurisdiction, consider recording abusive incidents. Make sure to understand the laws regarding recording conversations in your area.
2. **Voicemails:** Save any threatening or abusive voicemails.

Financial Records

1. **Bank Statements:** Keep copies of bank statements if your partner is controlling your finances.
2. **Receipts:** Save receipts that show financial control, such as your

partner only giving you a small allowance.

How to Safely Store Evidence

Safely storing your evidence is crucial to ensure it's accessible when you need it without alerting your abuser. Here are some tips:

1. **Digital Copies:** Store digital copies of evidence in a secure, cloud-based service that your partner cannot access. Google Drive, Dropbox, or a dedicated app like DocuSafe can be useful.
2. **Backup:** Have multiple backups of your digital evidence, possibly stored on an external drive that's kept in a secure location.
3. **Trusted Person:** Consider giving copies of your evidence to a trusted friend, family member, or lawyer who can keep it safe for you.
4. **Password Protection:** Use strong, unique passwords for any online accounts where you store evidence. Ensure these passwords are not known to your partner.

Creating a Documentation Plan

1. **Regular Updates:** Make documenting incidents a regular habit. Set aside time each day or week to update your records.
2. **Detail-Oriented:** Be as detailed as possible. Include the context of each incident, what was said, how you felt, and any aftermath.
3. **Organized:** Keep your evidence organized by date and type. This will make it easier to reference specific incidents later on.

Seeking Professional Help

Gathering evidence can be overwhelming and emotionally taxing. Don't hesitate to seek professional help:

1. **Counselors:** A therapist or counselor can help you process your experiences and provide emotional support.
2. **Legal Advice:** Consult with a lawyer who specializes in domestic abuse cases. They can guide you on what evidence will be most useful and how to gather it safely.
3. **Support Groups:** Join a support group for people experiencing domestic abuse. Sharing your experiences with others who understand can be incredibly validating and empowering.

Moving Forward

As you gather your wits and evidence, you're taking powerful steps towards reclaiming your life. This process might feel daunting, but each piece of evidence you collect is a step towards freedom and justice. Remember, you are not alone, and there are many resources and people ready to support you through this journey.

Conclusion

Gathering evidence is a critical part of preparing to leave an abusive relationship. It's about more than just collecting proof; it's about reclaiming your power, validating your experiences, and building a solid foundation for your legal and emotional journey ahead. Channel your inner detective, document everything meticulously, and keep your evidence safe. This preparation will arm you with the tools you need to protect yourself and start anew. Remember, you have the strength and courage to take these steps, and you deserve a life free from abuse.

Creating an exit strategy is vital. It doesn't have to be as dramatic as disappearing in a puff of smoke, but it should be well thought out. Planning where you'll go, what you'll take, and how you'll get there is crucial for ensuring your safety and success. This chapter will guide you through developing a comprehensive exit plan.

Assessing Your Situation

Before you start planning your exit, assess your current situation:

1. **Danger Level:** Determine the immediate danger you're in. If you're in imminent danger, prioritize finding a safe place immediately.
2. **Timing:** Consider the best time to leave. Look for a window of opportunity when your partner is least likely to notice, such as when they are at work or out of town.
3. **Resources:** Identify what resources you currently have and what you'll need. This includes financial resources, documents, transportation, and support networks.

Step 6
Develop Your Exit Strategy
(Because Smoke Bombs Are for Ninjas)

Step 1: Identify a Safe Destination

Find a place where you can go that your partner won't suspect. This could be a friend or family member's house, a domestic violence shelter, or a safe house.

- **Domestic Violence Shelters:** Many shelters offer confidential locations and support services. Research shelters in your area and keep their contact information handy.
- **Friends and Family:** If it's safe, consider staying with a trusted friend or family member. Ensure they understand the need for secrecy and safety.

Step 2: Gather Essential Documents

Collect important documents that you'll need after you leave. These include:

- **Identification:** Driver's license, passport, birth certificates for you and your children.
- **Financial Documents:** Bank statements, credit cards, checkbooks, investment records.
- **Legal Documents:** Marriage certificate, any protective orders, custody papers, insurance policies.
- **Medical Records:** Immunization records, prescription information, health insurance cards.

Keep these documents in a secure, easily accessible place. Consider storing copies digitally in a password-protected cloud service.

Step 3: Prepare an Emergency Bag

Pack an emergency bag with essential items you'll need for the first few days after you leave. Keep this bag hidden but easily accessible. Include:

- **Clothing:** Pack enough clothing for a few days for yourself and your children.
- **Money:** Include cash, prepaid cards, and any financial resources you can access.
- **Keys:** House keys, car keys, and any other keys you might need.
- **Medications:** Include any prescription medications and over-the-counter essentials.
- **Electronics:** A burner phone if possible, phone charger, and a laptop or tablet if necessary.
- **Personal Items:** Toiletries, sentimental items, and anything else

essential for your well-being.

Step 4: Plan Your Transportation

Figure out how you will leave and what transportation you will use:

- **Own Vehicle:** If you have your own car, ensure it's fueled and ready to go. Park it in a place that's easy to access quickly.
- **Public Transportation:** Know the schedules and routes of buses, trains, or other public transport options.
- **Rideshare Services:** Consider using rideshare services like Uber or Lyft if you don't have access to a car.
- **Friends or Family:** Arrange for someone you trust to pick you up at a pre-determined time and place.

Step 5: Create a Safety Plan

A safety plan outlines how to leave and stay safe once you've left. Include:

- **Communication Plan:** Decide how you will communicate with trusted people once you've left. Establish safe words or signals if necessary.
- **Legal Protection:** If you haven't already, seek a restraining order or protective order to keep your partner away.
- **Post-Exit Plan:** Plan where you will go after your initial safe place and how you will maintain your safety. This might include changing your phone number, getting a new place to live, or altering your routine.

Practicing Your Exit Strategy

Practice your exit strategy to ensure everything goes smoothly when the time comes:

- **Dry Runs:** Conduct dry runs of your exit plan. Leave the house with your emergency bag, get to your vehicle, and drive to your safe place. This practice can help you identify and address potential issues.
- **Children and Pets:** If you have children or pets, make sure they are part of the practice runs. Ensure they know what to do and where to go.

Seeking Support

Leaving an abusive relationship is challenging, but support is available:

- **Support Groups:** Join support groups for survivors of domestic abuse. Sharing your experiences and hearing others' stories can provide emotional support and practical advice.
- **Hotlines:** Use domestic violence hotlines for immediate support and guidance. They can connect you with local resources and offer crisis intervention.
- **Counseling:** Seek counseling to help you process your experiences and plan for the future. Many organizations offer free or low-cost services for survivors.

After You Leave

Once you've left, it's important to stay safe and start rebuilding your life:

1. **Legal Actions:** Follow through with any legal actions, such as restraining orders or custody arrangements.
2. **Financial Independence:** Work towards financial

independence. Open your own bank account, seek employment if you're not already working, and create a budget.

3. **New Routine:** Establish a new routine that minimizes the risk of your partner finding you. This might include changing your daily habits, moving to a new location, and using new social circles.

Conclusion

Developing a comprehensive exit strategy is crucial for leaving an abusive relationship safely. By carefully planning where you'll go, what you'll take, and how you'll get there, you increase your chances of a successful escape. Remember, this process might be challenging, but with determination and support, you can achieve freedom and rebuild your life. Stay focused, stay safe, and take each step with confidence, knowing that you deserve a life free from abuse.

Chapter 7

Build Your Support Squad (Yes, Even Your Cat Counts)

Surrounding yourself with a supportive network is crucial as you prepare to leave an abusive relationship. Friends, family, therapists – even your cat – can play an essential role in providing the emotional and practical support you need. Building a strong support system will give you the strength to follow through with your plans and start anew. This chapter will guide you through the process of assembling your support squad.

Why a Support Squad is Essential

Leaving an abusive relationship is one of the most challenging things you can do. A support squad can provide:

1. **Emotional Support:** Encouragement, understanding, and a listening ear.
2. **Practical Help:** Assistance with logistics, such as transportation, childcare, and temporary housing.
3. **Safety and Security:** Protection and a safe environment where you can regroup and plan your next steps.
4. **Accountability:** Motivation and reminders to stay committed to your plan.

Identifying Your Allies

Friends and Family

Start by identifying friends and family members who you trust and who understand your situation. Not everyone in your social circle will be supportive or understand the complexities of abuse, so choose wisely:

- **Trustworthy Individuals:** Select people who have proven to be reliable and non-judgmental.
- **Good Listeners:** Choose friends and family who are empathetic and willing to listen without giving unsolicited advice.
- **Practical Helpers:** Look for people who can offer practical support, such as a place to stay, transportation, or help with finances.

Professional Support

Professional support can provide expertise and confidentiality that friends and family might not be able to offer:

- **Therapists and Counselors:** Seek out therapists who specialize in domestic abuse. They can help you process your experiences and develop coping strategies.
- **Support Groups:** Join support groups for domestic abuse survivors. Sharing your story and hearing others can provide validation and encouragement.
- **Legal Advisors:** A lawyer specializing in domestic violence can provide critical legal advice and help you navigate the legal system.

Community Resources

Community organizations can offer various forms of support:

- **Domestic Violence Shelters:** Shelters provide a safe place to stay and often offer additional services like counseling and legal assistance.
- **Hotlines:** Domestic violence hotlines can provide immediate

support and connect you with local resources.

- **Nonprofits and NGOs:** Organizations dedicated to helping domestic abuse survivors can offer a range of services, from financial assistance to job training.

- **Routine and Normalcy:** Caring for a pet provides a sense of routine and purpose, which can help stabilize your life during chaotic periods.
- **Safety Concerns:** If you have a pet, plan for their safety as well. Many shelters and organizations can help with temporary pet care if needed.

Steps to Build Your Support Squad

Step 1: Reach Out

Start reaching out to potential members of your support squad. Be honest about your situation and what you need from them. It might be difficult to share your experiences, but honesty is crucial for receiving the right kind of support.

- **Direct Conversations:** Have direct conversations with friends and family members. Explain your situation and how they can help.
- **Confidentiality:** Emphasize the importance of keeping your plans confidential to ensure your safety.

Step 2: Establish a Communication Plan

Set up a reliable and secure way to communicate with your support squad:

- **Safe Communication Methods:** Use secure communication methods, such as encrypted messaging apps like Signal, to discuss sensitive information.
- **Code Words:** Establish code words or phrases that can indicate when you need immediate help or when it's safe to talk.

Step 3: Create a Support Schedule

Organize a schedule for practical support. This can include:

- **Transportation:** Arrange for someone to provide transportation when you decide to leave.
- **Temporary Housing:** Confirm who can offer you a place to stay and for how long.
- **Childcare:** If you have children, arrange for trusted individuals to help with childcare during the transition.

Step 4: Regular Check-ins

Maintain regular check-ins with your support squad to keep them updated on your situation and progress:

- **Weekly Calls/Meetings:** Set up weekly calls or meetings with key members of your support squad to discuss your progress and any new developments.
- **Emergency Contacts:** Ensure that key members of your support squad know how to contact each other in case of an emergency.

Emotional and Psychological Support

Dealing with the emotional and psychological impact of leaving an abusive relationship is challenging. Lean on your support squad for:

- **Therapeutic Support:** Regular sessions with a therapist can provide ongoing emotional support and strategies to cope with anxiety, fear, and trauma.
- **Support Groups:** Participate in support groups to share your experiences and gain strength from others who have been through similar situations.
- **Positive Reinforcement:** Encourage friends and family to offer positive reinforcement, helping to boost your confidence and self-esteem.

Self-Care and Personal Empowerment

While your support squad is vital, don't forget to take care of yourself:

- **Self-Care Routine:** Establish a self-care routine that includes activities that relax and rejuvenate you, such as exercise, reading, or meditation.
- **Personal Goals:** Set personal goals that focus on your well-being and independence, such as finding a new job, furthering your education, or developing new hobbies.
- **Celebrate Small Wins:** Acknowledge and celebrate small victories along the way. Each step towards independence and safety is an achievement.

Moving Forward

Building your support squad is a critical step in preparing to leave an abusive relationship. It provides the emotional, practical, and psychological support necessary to navigate this challenging time.

Remember, you are not alone. By surrounding yourself with caring and supportive individuals, you create a safety net that will help you through the process of leaving and rebuilding your life.

Conclusion

Developing a strong support squad is essential for successfully leaving an abusive relationship. Friends, family, professionals, community resources, and even your pets can provide the encouragement, practical help, and emotional strength you need. Take the time to build and nurture this network, ensuring you have a solid foundation as you take steps towards a safer, happier future. You deserve to be surrounded by love, respect, and support – and with a strong support squad, you can achieve that.

Chapter 8

Financial Independence: Embrace Your Inner Boss

Achieving financial independence is a critical step in leaving an abusive relationship and reclaiming your life. Financial control is often a significant tool of abuse, keeping you dependent and trapped. By taking steps to secure your own financial stability, you not only gain the resources needed to leave but also build the confidence and autonomy that are essential for your freedom. This chapter will guide you through practical steps to embrace your inner boss and achieve financial independence.

Why Financial Independence is Essential

Financial independence empowers you to make decisions about your life without relying on your abuser. It gives you the means to support yourself and your children, secure housing, and cover legal and medical expenses. Most importantly, it provides the foundation for a new life where you are in control.

Steps to Achieve Financial Independence

Step 1: Assess Your Current Financial Situation

Start by understanding your current financial status:

- **Income:** Identify all sources of income, including wages, benefits, child support, and any other financial support.
- **Expenses:** List all your expenses, including housing, utilities, food, transportation, childcare, and debts.

- **Assets:** Determine what assets you have, such as savings accounts, investments, property, or valuable items.
- **Debts:** Note any debts you owe, including credit card balances, loans, and any other financial obligations.

Step 2: Open a Separate Bank Account

Having a separate bank account is essential for ensuring that you have control over your finances:

- **Choose a Safe Bank:** Select a bank that your partner doesn't use to avoid any potential monitoring.
- **Keep it Confidential:** Use a secure address, such as a PO box or a trusted friend's address, to receive bank statements and correspondence.
- **Online Banking:** Set up online banking for easy access and management of your account.

Step 3: Start Saving Money

Building a financial cushion is crucial for your transition to independence:

- **Emergency Fund:** Aim to save enough money to cover at least three months of living expenses. This fund will provide a safety net in case of emergencies.
- **Small Contributions:** Start small if necessary. Even small amounts saved regularly can add up over time.
- **Cash Stash:** If opening a bank account is not immediately feasible, start stashing cash in a secure, undisclosed location.

Step 4: Secure Employment

Having a stable source of income is vital for financial independence:

- **Job Search:** Begin looking for a job if you don't already have one. Utilize job search websites, local classifieds, and community bulletin boards.
- **Skills and Training:** Consider furthering your education or acquiring new skills to enhance your employability. Many community centers and organizations offer free or low-cost training programs.
- **Part-Time or Freelance Work:** If full-time employment is not immediately possible, consider part-time or freelance work to start generating income.

Step 5: Manage and Protect Your Finances

Once you have a separate account and a source of income, it's crucial to manage and protect your finances:

- **Budgeting:** Create a budget that outlines your income and expenses. Prioritize essential expenses and savings.
- **Credit Protection:** Monitor your credit report regularly for any unauthorized activity. Consider placing a fraud alert or credit freeze if necessary.
- **Financial Literacy:** Educate yourself about personal finance. Resources such as books, online courses, and financial counseling can help you manage your money effectively.

Additional Financial Resources

Explore additional resources that can provide financial support:

- **Government Assistance:** Research government programs that offer financial assistance, such as housing subsidies, food stamps, and childcare support.
- **Nonprofits and Charities:** Many organizations provide financial aid to individuals fleeing abusive relationships. Look for grants, emergency funds, and support services in your area.
- **Community Resources:** Local community centers often have resources and programs to help with job placement, financial planning, and other support services.

Building a Financial Support Network

In addition to practical steps, building a network of financial support can be invaluable:

- **Financial Advisors:** Seek advice from financial advisors who can help you plan and manage your finances.
- **Support Groups:** Join support groups for survivors of domestic abuse, where you can share resources and financial tips.
- **Trusted Individuals:** Rely on trusted friends or family members who can provide financial guidance and support.

Embracing Your Inner Boss

Achieving financial independence is not just about money; it's about embracing your inner boss and taking control of your life:

- **Confidence:** Building financial independence will boost your confidence and self-esteem. Every step you take towards managing your finances is a step towards empowerment.
- **Autonomy:** Financial independence means you can make decisions about your life without relying on someone else. This

autonomy is crucial for your sense of freedom and control.

- **Future Planning:** With financial independence, you can start planning for your future, setting goals, and working towards a life that you desire and deserve.

Moving Forward

Embracing your inner boss and achieving financial independence is a journey that requires time, effort, and determination. Each step you take brings you closer to a life where you are in control. Remember, you deserve to live free from abuse and with the financial stability to support yourself and your dreams.

Conclusion

Financial independence is a cornerstone of freedom from an abusive relationship. By opening a separate bank account, saving money, securing a job, and managing your finances, you can build a strong foundation for your new life. Embrace your inner boss and take control of your financial future, knowing that each step you take is a step towards empowerment and autonomy. You have the strength and capability to achieve financial independence and create the life you deserve.

Chapter 9

The Dreaded "C" Word: Counseling and Therapy

Therapy isn't a dirty word. Seeking counseling can be one of the most empowering decisions you make on your journey to healing and rebuilding your life. Professional help can provide you with the tools needed to navigate your emotions, rebuild your self-esteem, and move forward. This chapter will guide you through understanding the importance of therapy, how to find the right counselor, and what to expect from the process.

Understanding the Importance of Counseling and Therapy

Therapy can offer numerous benefits for those recovering from an abusive relationship:

1. **Emotional Healing:** Therapy provides a safe space to process your emotions and experiences. It helps you understand and manage feelings of anger, sadness, fear, and confusion.
2. **Rebuilding Self-Esteem:** Abusive relationships often erode self-esteem and self-worth. Therapy can help you rebuild a positive self-image and develop self-confidence.
3. **Coping Strategies:** Therapists can teach you practical coping strategies to deal with anxiety, stress, and triggers related to your past experiences.
4. **Understanding Patterns:** Therapy can help you recognize and understand patterns of behavior and thought that have been influenced by the abuse, allowing you to break free from them.
5. **Empowerment:** Counseling empowers you to take control of your life, make healthier choices, and set boundaries.

Finding the Right Counselor

Finding the right counselor is crucial for effective therapy. Here are some steps to help you find a professional who meets your needs:

Step 1: Identify Your Needs

Determine what you're looking for in a therapist:

- **Specialization:** Look for a therapist who specializes in domestic abuse, trauma, and post-traumatic stress disorder (PTSD).
- **Approach:** Consider what type of therapeutic approach might work best for you, such as cognitive-behavioral therapy (CBT), dialectical behavior therapy (DBT), or trauma-focused therapy.
- **Gender and Cultural Sensitivity:** Choose a therapist with whom you feel comfortable, and who understands your cultural background and gender-specific issues.

Step 2: Research and Referrals

Use various resources to find potential therapists:

- **Referrals:** Ask for referrals from friends, family, or support groups who have had positive experiences with therapy.
- **Online Directories:** Use online directories such as Psychology Today, TherapyDen, or GoodTherapy to search for therapists in your area.
- **Local Resources:** Contact local domestic violence shelters, community centers, or medical professionals for recommendations.

Step 3: Initial Consultation

Schedule an initial consultation with potential therapists to determine if they are a good fit:

- **Questions to Ask:** Inquire about their experience with domestic abuse survivors, their therapeutic approach, and their availability.
- **Trust Your Instincts:** Pay attention to how you feel during the consultation. It's important to feel comfortable and safe with your therapist.

What to Expect from Therapy

Understanding what to expect from therapy can help you feel more comfortable and prepared:

The First Session

The first session typically involves:

- **Assessment:** Your therapist will ask about your background, current situation, and specific issues you want to address.
- **Goal Setting:** Together, you'll set goals for your therapy, focusing on what you hope to achieve.
- **Building Rapport:** This initial session is also about building a rapport and establishing trust with your therapist.

Ongoing Sessions

As therapy progresses, you can expect:

- **Exploration of Emotions:** You'll delve into your emotions and experiences, exploring how the abuse has impacted you.

- **Skill Development:** Your therapist will teach you coping skills and strategies to manage anxiety, stress, and other symptoms.
- **Behavioral Change:** Therapy will help you identify and change negative thought patterns and behaviors influenced by the abuse.
- **Empowerment:** Over time, therapy will empower you to make positive changes, set boundaries, and take control of your life.

Overcoming Common Barriers to Therapy

Many people hesitate to seek therapy due to various barriers. Here's how to overcome them:

Stigma

There is often a stigma attached to seeking therapy, but it's important to remember that taking care of your mental health is a sign of strength, not weakness.

Cost

Therapy can be expensive, but there are options:

- **Sliding Scale Fees:** Many therapists offer sliding scale fees based on your income.
- **Insurance:** Check if your insurance covers mental health services.
- **Community Resources:** Look for community organizations that offer free or low-cost counseling services.

Fear of Judgment

It's natural to fear judgment, but therapists are trained to be non-judgmental and supportive. They provide a safe space for you to express yourself without fear of criticism.

Alternative and Complementary Therapies

In addition to traditional talk therapy, consider alternative and complementary therapies that can aid in your healing:

- **Group Therapy:** Joining a support group for domestic abuse survivors can provide community and shared experiences.
- **Art and Music Therapy:** These therapies allow you to express your emotions creatively and can be very therapeutic.
- **Mindfulness and Meditation:** Practices like mindfulness and meditation can help reduce stress and improve emotional regulation.
- **Exercise and Physical Activity:** Regular exercise can boost your mood, reduce anxiety, and improve overall well-being.

Moving Forward

Seeking counseling and therapy is a crucial step in your journey to healing and independence. Embrace the process, knowing that it's a powerful tool for reclaiming your life and building a healthier future. With the support of a skilled therapist, you can navigate your emotions, rebuild your self-esteem, and develop the resilience needed to move forward.

Conclusion

Therapy isn't a dirty word; it's a lifeline. By seeking counseling, you're taking an essential step towards healing and empowerment. Professional help can provide the tools you need to navigate your emotions, rebuild your self-esteem, and move forward. Remember, you are not alone, and seeking help is a sign of strength. Embrace the journey of therapy and counseling, and take control of your healing process, knowing that you deserve a life of peace, happiness, and freedom.

Chapter 10

Execute Your Plan: How to Walk Out with Style

When the time comes, walk out with your head held high. Execute your plan with precision. Remember, you're not just leaving an abuser; you're reclaiming your life. This chapter will provide you with the insights and strategies needed to leave your abusive relationship with confidence and style, ensuring that you are prepared, empowered, and ready for a new beginning.

Preparation is Key

The key to executing your plan effectively is thorough preparation. Here's how to ensure you're ready:

1. Finalize Your Exit Strategy

By now, you should have a well-thought-out exit plan (refer back to Chapter 6). Review your plan to ensure everything is in place:

- **Safe Destination:** Confirm your safe place, whether it's with a friend, family member, or a domestic violence shelter.
- **Emergency Bag:** Double-check that your emergency bag contains all essential items, including identification, financial resources, medications, and personal items.
- **Transportation:** Ensure you have reliable transportation arranged, whether it's your own vehicle, public transportation, or a ride from a trusted person.

2. Gather and Secure Your Evidence

Ensure all evidence of the abuse is securely stored and easily accessible. This includes photographs, medical records, journals, and any other documentation that may be needed for legal purposes.

3. Notify Your Support Squad

Alert your support squad (as discussed in Chapter 7) that the time has come. Ensure they are ready to provide the assistance you need, whether it's emotional support, transportation, or a safe place to stay.

The Day of Departure

When the day arrives, it's important to stay calm, focused, and determined. Here's a step-by-step guide to executing your plan:

1. Choose the Right Moment

Select a moment when your partner is not around or is least likely to suspect anything. This could be when they are at work, out with friends, or otherwise occupied.

2. Execute Quickly and Efficiently

Speed and efficiency are crucial. Once you've decided to leave, act swiftly to minimize the risk of confrontation or being stopped:

- **Collect Your Belongings:** Gather your emergency bag and any last-minute items.
- **Exit Quietly:** Leave the house quietly to avoid drawing attention. If you have children or pets, ensure they are ready and know the plan.

3. Contact Your Support Squad

As soon as you are safely away from the immediate danger, contact your support squad to let them know you've left and are on your way to your safe destination.

Handling Confrontation

If you encounter your partner or face confrontation during your departure, prioritize your safety:

- **Stay Calm:** Keep your composure and avoid engaging in arguments.
- **Have a Quick Exit Plan:** Be ready to leave immediately if the situation escalates.
- **Call for Help:** Don't hesitate to call the police if you feel threatened or unsafe.

Immediate Steps After Leaving

Once you've left, there are several important steps to take to ensure your ongoing safety and begin your new life:

1. Secure Your Location

Upon arrival at your safe destination, take steps to secure it:

- **Privacy:** Ensure your location remains confidential. Inform only trusted individuals of your whereabouts.
- **Security Measures:** Implement security measures such as changing locks, securing windows, and setting up a security system if possible.

2. Notify Authorities

Consider notifying the police of your situation, especially if you have left with children. This creates an official record and can provide additional protection.

3. Seek Legal Protection

If you haven't already, seek legal protection such as a restraining order or protective order. Consult with a legal professional to understand your rights and options.

Rebuilding Your Life

Leaving is just the first step. Rebuilding your life requires time, effort, and support. Here are some insights on moving forward with style and confidence:

1. Focus on Self-Care

Prioritize your physical and emotional well-being:

- **Therapy and Counseling:** Continue with therapy to process your experiences and build resilience.
- **Healthy Routine:** Establish a routine that includes regular exercise, healthy eating, and sufficient rest.
- **Relaxation Techniques:** Practice relaxation techniques such as mindfulness, meditation, or yoga to manage stress and anxiety.

2. Establish Financial Independence

Work towards financial independence as discussed in Chapter 8:

- **Secure Employment:** Find stable employment or further your education to improve your job prospects.
- **Financial Planning:** Create a budget, save money, and manage your finances responsibly.

3. Build a Supportive Community

Surround yourself with positive and supportive people:

- **Reconnect with Friends and Family:** Rebuild relationships with friends and family members who support your new life.
- **Join Support Groups:** Engage with support groups for domestic abuse survivors to share experiences and gain strength from others.

4. Set New Goals

Define new goals for your future and take steps to achieve them:

- **Personal Development:** Pursue hobbies, interests, and activities that bring you joy and fulfillment.
- **Education and Career:** Set educational and career goals that align with your aspirations and work towards achieving them.
- **Empowerment:** Embrace opportunities for personal growth and empowerment.

Celebrating Your Courage

Leaving an abusive relationship is a monumental act of courage. Celebrate your bravery and acknowledge the strength it took to reclaim your life:

- **Small Wins:** Celebrate small victories along the way, whether it's securing a job, completing a therapy session, or simply feeling happier.

- **Affirmations:** Use positive affirmations to reinforce your self-worth and remind yourself of your strength and resilience.

Conclusion

Executing your plan to leave an abusive relationship is a bold and courageous step towards reclaiming your life. By preparing thoroughly, acting swiftly, and focusing on your future, you can leave with confidence and style. Remember, you are not just leaving an abuser; you are stepping into a future filled with hope, freedom, and endless possibilities. Embrace this new chapter with your head held high, knowing that you have the strength and determination to build the life you deserve.

The Gospel of Jesus: Declaring Freedom and Liberty93 for Women

The spirit of God is upon me to declare captives free and announce the year of liberty to women. This treatise seeks to eliminate all unfounded religious manipulations that keep religious women in abusive relationships. It is inspired by the teachings of Jesus Christ, who championed love, respect, and dignity for all individuals, and stands against any form of oppression and abuse.

Jesus' Mission: Freedom and Liberation

In Luke 4:18-19, Jesus declared His mission: "The Spirit of the Lord is upon me, because he has anointed me to proclaim good news to the poor. He has sent me to proclaim freedom for the prisoners and recovery of sight for the blind, to set the oppressed free, to proclaim the year of the Lord's favor." This powerful proclamation sets the foundation for understanding Jesus' stance on freedom and liberation, particularly for women who are oppressed and abused.

Jesus and Women: A Testament to Equality and Dignity

Throughout His ministry, Jesus consistently elevated the status of women, treating them with respect and dignity, countering the cultural norms of His time. Here are some key examples:

The Samaritan Woman (John 4:1-42)

In His conversation with the Samaritan woman at the well, Jesus broke several societal taboos. He spoke to her directly, acknowledged her worth, and offered her the living water of eternal life. This encounter highlights Jesus' willingness to reach out to marginalized women and affirm their value.

The Woman Caught in Adultery (John 8:1-11)

When a woman caught in adultery was brought to Jesus, He defended her against those who sought to stone her. Jesus said, "Let any one of you who is without sin be the first to throw a stone at her." His response emphasized mercy, forgiveness, and the inherent dignity of the woman, rather than condemnation and punishment.

Mary and Martha (Luke 10:38-42)

Jesus' interaction with Mary and Martha demonstrates His recognition of women's spiritual capacity and right to learn. When Martha complained that Mary was not helping with household duties, Jesus affirmed Mary's choice to sit at His feet and learn, saying, "Mary has chosen what is better, and it will not be taken away from her."

Addressing Religious Manipulations

Religious manipulations that justify abuse and oppression are antithetical to the teachings of Jesus. Here, we address and refute some common manipulations:

Misinterpretation of Submission

Ephesians 5:22 is often cited: "Wives, submit yourselves to your own husbands as you do to the Lord." However, this verse must be understood in its full context. Ephesians 5:21 precedes it with, "Submit to one another out of reverence for Christ." Mutual submission, love, and respect are the true essence of this passage. Husbands are called to love their wives as Christ loved the church (Ephesians 5:25), which means sacrificially and without abuse.

The Role of Suffering

Some argue that women should endure suffering in marriage as a form of righteousness. This is a misapplication of scripture. While Jesus speaks about taking up our crosses (Matthew 16:24), this does not imply enduring abuse. The call to follow Jesus is about living a life of love, justice, and peace, not suffering at the hands of another.

Divorce and Remarriage

Religious teachings on divorce can sometimes trap women in abusive marriages. However, Jesus' teachings on divorce (Matthew 19:3-9) focus on the sanctity of marriage but also acknowledge human fallibility. The well-being and safety of individuals are paramount. In cases of abuse, the spirit of Jesus' teachings supports the protection and dignity of the oppressed over the rigid enforcement of legalistic interpretations.

Proclaiming the Year of Liberty

It is time to proclaim the year of the Lord's favor for women trapped in abusive relationships. Here are steps to embrace this liberation:

Recognize Your Worth

Women must recognize their inherent worth and dignity. You are created in the image of God (Genesis 1:27) and deserve to be treated with respect and love.

Oh, Marriage

Oh, marriage. That divine institution allegedly designed by God to trap souls in lifelong contracts. Because, of course, the Almighty, in all His glory, would be so desperate for followers that He'd employ the bait of matrimony. Never mind the fact that there's no record of a "Christian" or "biblical" marriage anywhere in the sacred texts—details, details.

Let's also dispel the delightful myth that God expects people to endure abusive marriages as some sort of sacrificial offering. Really, the Creator of the Universe, who could snap His fingers to populate the Earth with devout worshippers, needs you to stay miserable to prove your devotion? Preposterous.

Women, hold on to your seats, because here's the shocker: you actually have the right to choose your relationships! That's right—freedom and dignity are not contrary to God's will. Walking out of a toxic relationship won't incur divine wrath; in fact, it might just be the most sensible, God-honoring thing you do.

And speaking of brave souls, let's pay homage to the heroine and brave Rachael Nyarangi. Rachael, you went through unnecessary pain and did more than any ordinary lady would do to make your marriage work. You remain a testament to a woman's resilience, defying any man's stupidity in his wish that you go an extra mile chasing empty clouds. In your honor, I have written this book.

So, in summary, if you believe that God needs your misery to recruit followers, or that He's the architect of a marriage model that demands suffering, perhaps it's time to reconsider what kind of deity you're worshipping. Spoiler alert: it's not the benevolent one. Instead, let's celebrate the resilience and strength of women like Rachael, who remind us that endurance of suffering is not a divine mandate but a human travesty.

Chapter 11

Reinventing Yourself: You're Free! Now What?

Congratulations, you're free! The moment you've been waiting for has finally arrived. Now, it's time to reinvent yourself, explore new hobbies, meet new people, and rediscover your passions. This is your chance to create the life you deserve. This chapter will guide you through the exciting journey of reinventing yourself and embracing the opportunities that lie ahead.

Embracing Your Freedom

Freedom from an abusive relationship is both exhilarating and daunting. It's a time of transition, self-discovery, and growth. Here's how to start embracing your new life:

1. Celebrate Your Freedom

Acknowledge and celebrate your courage and resilience. You've made it through an incredibly challenging period, and you deserve to recognize your achievement.

- **Mark the Occasion:** Celebrate in a way that feels meaningful to you, whether it's a small gathering with friends, a special outing, or simply a quiet moment of reflection.
- **Self-Recognition:** Write down your journey, the challenges you overcame, and the strengths you discovered in yourself. Keep this as a reminder of your resilience.

Rediscovering Your Passions

One of the most exciting aspects of reinventing yourself is rediscovering your passions and interests. Here's how to embark on this journey:

1. Explore New Hobbies

Take this opportunity to try new activities and hobbies. Experiment with different interests until you find what truly brings you joy.

- **Creative Pursuits:** Explore artistic activities such as painting, writing, music, or crafting. Creativity can be a powerful outlet for self-expression and healing.
- **Physical Activities:** Engage in physical activities like dancing, yoga, hiking, or joining a sports team. Physical exercise not only boosts your mood but also improves your overall health.
- **Learning Opportunities:** Consider taking classes or workshops in subjects that interest you, whether it's cooking, photography, gardening, or a new language.

2. Reconnect with Old Interests

Think back to hobbies or interests you had before your relationship. Reconnecting with these can be a powerful way to reclaim parts of yourself that may have been suppressed.

- **Reflect:** Spend time reflecting on what activities used to make you happy and fulfilled.
- **Reengage:** Find local groups, clubs, or classes that focus on these interests and start participating.

Building a New Social Network

Meeting new people and building a supportive social network is crucial for your reinvention. Surrounding yourself with positive and encouraging individuals will help you thrive.

1. Join Social Groups

Seek out social groups or clubs that align with your interests and values. This can be a great way to meet like-minded individuals and form new friendships.

- **Community Centers:** Check out local community centers for groups and activities that interest you.
- **Online Communities:** Join online forums or social media groups related to your hobbies and passions.

2. Volunteer

Volunteering is a rewarding way to give back to your community, meet new people, and gain a sense of purpose.

- **Local Charities:** Find local charities or organizations that resonate with you and offer your time and skills.
- **Events and Fundraisers:** Participate in community events and fundraisers to expand your network and make a positive impact.

3. Reconnect with Positive People

Rebuild relationships with friends and family members who are supportive and positive influences in your life.

- **Reach Out:** Don't hesitate to reach out to old friends or family members you may have lost touch with.

- **Build Trust:** Take time to rebuild trust and strengthen these relationships.

Focusing on Personal Growth

Personal growth is a continuous journey. Embrace opportunities for self-improvement and empowerment.

Set New Goals

1. Setting goals gives you direction and a sense of purpose. Focus on what you want to achieve in various aspects of your life.

- **Short-Term Goals:** Set achievable short-term goals to build momentum and confidence.
- **Long-Term Goals:** Define long-term goals that reflect your aspirations and dreams. Break them down into manageable steps.

2. Pursue Education and Career Advancement

Investing in your education and career can open new doors and provide financial independence.

- **Further Education:** Consider going back to school or taking courses to enhance your skills and knowledge.
- **Career Development:** Seek opportunities for career advancement, whether through job training, professional development, or exploring new career paths.

3. Practice Self-Care

Self-care is essential for maintaining your physical, emotional, and mental well-being.

- **Mindfulness and Meditation:** Practice mindfulness and meditation to reduce stress and enhance your emotional health.
- **Healthy Lifestyle:** Maintain a healthy lifestyle with balanced nutrition, regular exercise, and adequate sleep.
- **Therapeutic Activities:** Engage in activities that promote relaxation and self-care, such as reading, journaling, or taking baths.

Embracing New Opportunities

Your newfound freedom presents endless opportunities. Embrace them with an open heart and mind.

1. Travel and Adventure

Exploring new places and cultures can be incredibly liberating and enriching.

- **Local Exploration:** Start with local travel and discover hidden gems in your own area.
- **Broader Horizons:** Plan trips to places you've always wanted to visit. Travel can provide fresh perspectives and inspiration.

2. Take Risks

Don't be afraid to take risks and step out of your comfort zone. Growth often happens when you challenge yourself.

- **Try New Things:** Whether it's a new hobby, a new job, or a new relationship, be open to new experiences.
- **Embrace Change:** Accept that change is a natural part of life and an opportunity for growth.

Conclusion

Reinventing yourself after leaving an abusive relationship is a journey filled with possibilities and new beginnings. Embrace your freedom, rediscover your passions, build a supportive social network, and focus on personal growth. This is your chance to create the life you deserve, filled with joy, fulfillment, and endless opportunities. Celebrate your resilience and courage, and step into your new life with confidence and excitement. Remember, you are free, you are strong, and the best is yet to come.

Conclusion: Welcome to Your New Life

Walking out of an abusive marriage is no small feat, but you've done it. Welcome to your new life, where you are the hero of your own story. This journey has not been easy, and the courage, strength, and resilience you have shown are nothing short of extraordinary. As you step into this new chapter, embrace the freedom and endless possibilities that await you.

Celebrating Your Journey

Take a moment to reflect on the journey you've undertaken. You have faced immense challenges, made difficult decisions, and taken brave steps towards reclaiming your life. Each step, no matter how small, has been a testament to your strength and determination. Celebrate these victories, and recognize that you have already accomplished something incredible.

Embracing Your Freedom

Freedom is a powerful gift. It means having the ability to make your own choices, pursue your passions, and live life on your terms. Here's how to fully embrace and enjoy your newfound freedom:

- **Set Your Own Course:** Define what happiness and fulfillment mean to you. Set personal goals and take steps towards achieving them.
- **Explore New Horizons:** Whether it's traveling, trying new hobbies, or meeting new people, don't be afraid to explore and expand your world.
- **Take Care of Yourself:** Prioritize your physical, emotional, and mental well-being. Practice self-care regularly, and don't hesitate to seek support when needed.

Rebuilding and Reinventing

Rebuilding your life after leaving an abusive relationship involves rediscovering who you are and what you love. It's an opportunity to reinvent yourself and create the life you've always wanted:

- **Rediscover Your Passions:** Reconnect with old interests or discover new ones. Engaging in activities you love can bring joy and fulfillment.
- **Build a Supportive Network:** Surround yourself with positive and supportive people who encourage and uplift you.
- **Pursue Growth:** Continue to grow personally and professionally. Take advantage of opportunities for learning and development.

The Power of Humor and Sarcasm

Humor and sarcasm have been your allies throughout this journey, helping you cope with difficult situations and regain your sense of self. Continue to use them as tools to lighten the load and navigate life's challenges:

- **Lighten Up:** Don't forget to laugh. Humor can be a powerful way to relieve stress and bring perspective to challenging situations.
- **Empower Yourself:** Use sarcasm to assert your independence and strength. It's a reminder that you are in control and capable of overcoming anything.

Looking Forward

The future is bright and filled with possibilities. As you move forward, remember that you are not defined by your past but by the strength and resilience you've shown in overcoming it. Embrace each day with confidence and optimism, knowing that you have the power to shape your own destiny.

Staying Connected

Remember that you are not alone. Many resources and communities are available to support you as you continue your journey. Stay connected with support groups, counselors, and friends who understand and validate your experiences. Sharing your story and supporting others can also be a powerful way to heal and grow.

Final Thoughts

You've made it through one of the toughest battles, and now it's time to enjoy the freedom and happiness you deserve. Life is a journey, and while there will still be challenges, you have proven that you have the strength to overcome them. Welcome to your new life, where you are the hero, and every day is an opportunity to create something beautiful.

Embrace this new chapter with open arms, and never forget the incredible journey that brought you here. You are free, you are strong, and you are capable of achieving anything you set your mind to. Celebrate your freedom, cherish your journey, and look forward to the endless possibilities that await you. This is your life, and it's time to live it to the fullest.

Conclusion

Walking out of an abusive marriage is a monumental achievement, but it's just the beginning. Welcome to your new life, where you have the power to create the future you desire. Embrace your freedom, celebrate your resilience, and enjoy the journey ahead. You are the hero of your own story, and the best is yet to come.

When the Will of God Seems Bitter

Pain, suffering, and death lie at the heart of Human existence, becoming more apparent as we age. We don't dream of these harsh realities, except when a loved one battles illness or terminal disease. As we grow older, the depth of the world's cry becomes increasingly evident. The dust upon which we walk in many places is composed of the remains of men, women, and children. The world is full of grief and graves. The Bible says, "Every person knows the plague of their own hearts" (1 Kings 8:38). Most people carry an aching soul about something or someone. Every person knows the plague of their own heart.

Dealing with pain and suffering has always been a central issue in religion. What to do when the will of God seems bitter is crucial in every belief system. Various answers have been offered:

- **Islam** says to submit. It is the will of God; just accept it.
- **Buddhism** claims pain and suffering are our fault due to our desires.
- **Hedonism** advises avoiding it, though this is unsustainable.
- **Christian Science** advocates denial, which is itself painful and self-defeating.

Pain and suffering are real, and not even obedience to God will eliminate them. Eliminating pain and suffering is as impossible as eliminating sin in this world.

But what does Christianity say about pain and suffering? Christianity says to transform it. What Jesus did to the cross is what we need to do to pain and suffering. Jesus transfigured the Cross and turned it into the altar, the throne, and the door to paradise. As an altar, He offered Himself for the forgiveness of sin; as a throne, He offered paradise; and as a door to paradise, He broke down the barrier between a holy God and a sinful world, granting us access to the very heart of God.

But the cross and what it signifies was the bitterest cup that the Son of God had to drink. He drank our cup.

That is the point about every cross and every problem in life. There is no valuable lesson easily learned. It is easy to preach about penitence, but very hard to practice it. The answer to pain and suffering is not to deny it as Christian Science does, nor avoid it like Hedonism, nor blame oneself like Buddhism, nor unthinkingly submit as Islam teaches, but to transform it. In a world of freedom, where God respects human autonomy and never coerces, pain is inevitable. God never invented bombs and guns; human beings did. The pain caused by natural phenomena like earthquakes is not comparable to that caused by humans. Because we are free, pain and suffering are inevitable.

At the center of our faith is the cross. The willing acceptance of the cross by Jesus is the true secret of Christian living. It is easy to say it, but not easy to learn. I continually resist pain. God says to improve your character, and I insist mine is good—though it isn't, of course. We do all we can to avoid pain, but God says we must stay in the furnace until we are better. Pain and suffering will always exist. Why should it be otherwise? In this world, we commit all sorts of wrongs, including what we eat and drink. Some pain comes from our ignorance, others from being malicious and proud. Every human being has an old nature to fight, and because of it, mistakes are made and we reap the consequences in this life. If we hide under the merits of Christ, these mistakes and sins will not be held against us in eternity, but we must remember that even if David's sins were forgiven, he reaped consequences in this life. We must not become casual about sin because it is not held against us in eternity.

The cheerful acceptance of the will of God is the greatest lesson we have to learn. Crosses will come inevitably; it is mine to choose whether mine will be of brutal pain like the impenitent thief or whether my cross will be the staff of redemption like the penitent thief. There is no dodging pain in this life, no matter how prayerful we may be. You will lose a loved one, have financial problems, and be touched by pain anyhow and anywhere. God had one Son without sin but has never had a son or daughter without pain. Everything has two handles: if you take the wrong handle, it destroys you, but if you take the right handle, it lifts you. There is nothing so bad that if taken by the right handle cannot exalt, bless, and glorify. Just as a good thing taken by the wrong handle can destroy us. Which one of us would not like to be tempted by millions of Euros? We would all love the temptation, but some of us would be destroyed by it.

As we consider pain, we need to be reminded that when God started to create the world, He began with chaos. Desmond Ford has said, "Until you are broken you are useless." God cannot do anything with a person filled with self-confidence, self-righteousness, and pride in their own wisdom. God has to break us to make us. He often reduces us to nothing before He can make us something worthy.

We are to learn to look at pain as the birth travail of something wonderful. What birth ever took place without travail? I know no person in history ever used by God to bring people into the kingdom who did not go through the furnace. Only the wounded can minister to the wounded. God permits many things to happen to Christians not for their sake but for the sake of the people they will influence. We have more influence on people than any other person. And God will do many things to us to help that other person. There is nothing of worth ever achieved without pain. The cross always precedes the crown. Always the torn flesh before a glorified body. The crown of thorns before the crown of glory, dark Friday before Easter Sunday. There is no way of dodging the cross; it is the way home.

Shall we then dodge and complain? No, there is a sense in which when we look at the cross we say: Christ bore it for me and so I need not bear it. Rather we should discover the truth that because He bore the crown of thorns for me, these things that are so hard for me to take should work together for good. The wind that tosses the Atlantic of our lives, according to Spurgeon, is "all sent to waft our ship safely to the desired haven. Every wind that raises, soft or fierce, are divine monsoon harrying us on in the same direction of our soul's desire. God walks the tempest and rules the storm."

When we look at Christ bearing the crown of thorns we can say, despite the anxiety that tempts me, I need not let my mind be pierced by these trials because they have been baptized in the blood of Christ, they will work together for good because I love God (Romans 8:28). Paul had to learn it (2 Corinthians 12:8-9).

My friends, because we are sinful, unless we are under some pressures, we are prone to break out into more and more evil. It has been my experience that the days of trouble in my life do me more good than any sermon. I hate pain and I do what I can to avoid the inevitable. But I am comforted to know that he who is down need not fear for falling because he can fall no further. The valley of humiliation is a fruitful place. We never stay there. We walk through the valley of death. And we will abide in the house of God forever. We are not there in the valley forever, but in the house of God forever. All because the blood of Jesus washes away the sin and stain of those who believe.

There is no way to dodge pain, but we can baptize it. We can be sure of the promises of God that all things will work together for good to them that love Him. When the bitter water of Mara was experienced by the Israelites, Moses cried out and a branch was dipped into the water, and the bitter water became sweet. The remedy for all time when we find water very bitter is to dip the cross into our bitter experience. Realizing that it will sanctify and transform it and bring about an inevitable resurrection is the only answer when God's will seems bitter.

Thanks be to God for the assurance that neither death, nor life, nor angels, nor principalities, nor things present, nor things to come, nor powers, will be able to separate us from the love of God that is in Christ Jesus our Lord. Nothing can hurt us in a lasting sense, for one day God will take away all sorrows and wipe all tears away. And there will be that glorious land of far distances where we will see the Lamb in His beauty and cast our crowns at His feet and fill heaven with beautiful hallelujahs to Him who loved us and gave Himself for us. May God teach us to introduce the tree of life, the tree of the cross, whenever life's waters are bitter. May He continually point us to the resurrection day when we find ourselves on the cross, that we might sing, and like Daniel's worthies in the fiery furnace, realize that we lose nothing but our bonds, and then rise to walk in the fires accompanied by the Son of God. May God grant us that experience in every trial and trouble for Christ's sake.

Epilogue: The Fundamental Rights of Women

As you close this book, remember that your journey toward freedom and self-empowerment is rooted in your fundamental human rights. These rights are universal, inalienable, and inherent to every woman, regardless of cultural, religious, or societal norms. Understanding and embracing these rights is crucial as you continue to build a life of dignity, respect, and autonomy.

The Right to Live Free from Violence

Every woman has the right to live free from all forms of violence, including physical, emotional, psychological, and sexual abuse. No one has the right to harm or threaten you, and every instance of abuse is a violation of this fundamental right.

The Right to Equality

You have the right to be treated equally, without discrimination based on gender, race, ethnicity, religion, or any other characteristic. Equality means having the same opportunities, rights, and protections as anyone else.

The Right to Freedom and Autonomy

You have the right to make decisions about your own life, body, and future. This includes the freedom to choose your career, education, relationships, and all other aspects of your personal and professional life.

The Right to Education

Education is a powerful tool for personal and societal transformation. You have the right to access education and acquire knowledge that empowers you to pursue your goals and dreams.

The Right to Health

You have the right to access healthcare services that meet your needs, including reproductive health services. Your health and well-being are paramount, and you deserve to receive care and support without discrimination or stigma.

The Right to Work and Financial Independence

Every woman has the right to work in a safe and fair environment, to receive equal pay for equal work, and to achieve financial independence. This includes the right to own property, manage your finances, and pursue economic opportunities.

The Right to Participate in Public Life

You have the right to participate in the political, economic, and social life of your community and country. This includes the right to vote, run for office, and have your voice heard in all matters that affect you and your society.

The Right to Privacy

Your personal life, body, and choices are yours alone. You have the right to privacy and to make decisions without coercion or intrusion from others.

The Right to Seek Justice

If your rights are violated, you have the right to seek justice and accountability. This includes access to legal assistance, fair treatment in the justice system, and protection from retribution.

The Right to Dignity and Respect

Above all, you have the right to live with dignity and respect. You are deserving of love, kindness, and recognition of your inherent worth as a human being.

As you move forward, carry these rights with you as guiding principles. They are the foundation upon which you can build a life free from abuse and filled with opportunities for growth and happiness. Embrace your strength, pursue your passions, and never forget that you are worthy of all the rights and freedoms that humanity has to offer.

You are a powerful individual, capable of shaping your own destiny and contributing to a world where all women can live with dignity, equality, and freedom. Keep these rights close to your heart and let them inspire you to continue on your journey with courage and confidence.

Thank you for allowing this book to be a part of your journey. Here's to a future filled with endless possibilities and a life lived to its fullest.

With unwavering support and solidarity

1

Did you love *Grow a Backbone and Walk out of an Abusive Marriage*?
Then you should read *Hope and Healing: A Chaplain's Handbook*[1] by
Kayumba David!

[2]

As a survivor of a challenging illness, I have experienced firsthand the
profound impact that compassionate care can have on individuals in
their most vulnerable moments. My journey through a robust healthcare
environment in Belgium illuminated the critical role that various
professionals play in the healing process. Nurses, doctors, and countless
other healthcare staff dedicate themselves to the well-being of their
patients, often going above and beyond to ensure that each person feels
valued and cared for. Their unwavering commitment to service inspires
not only hope but also a sense of dignity during difficult times.

---

1. https://books2read.com/u/mg6dYX

2. https://books2read.com/u/mg6dYX

In writing this book, I am compelled to reflect on the significant contributions of those who serve in hospitals and other care settings, particularly chaplains who offer spiritual guidance and emotional support. They are the quiet yet powerful voices that provide comfort, instilling hope where despair often threatens to take root. Chaplains walk alongside patients and families, navigating the challenges of illness, suffering, and the uncertainty of life and death.

This guide aims to illuminate the path of chaplaincy in various environments, particularly within hospitals and prisons. It is a call to those who feel the tug of a sacred vocation, encouraging them to embrace their role as vessels of God's love and grace. It is my hope that this book serves as a source of inspiration and practical guidance for current and future chaplains, empowering them to foster healing, reconciliation, and transformation in the lives of those they serve.

May this work resonate with anyone who seeks to understand the beauty and importance of compassionate ministry, reminding us all of the profound difference that care and hope can make in our world.

Read more at www.zcews.org.